Celebrating Hispanic Culture

by Cynthia Downs

 Carson-Dellosa Publishing Company, Inc.
Greensboro, North Carolina

CREDITS

Editor: Sabena Maiden
Layout Design: Van Harris
Inside Illustrations: Jenny Campbell
Cover Design: Peggy Jackson
Cover Illustrations: Peggy Jackson

ISBN: 0-88724-921-3

Table of Contents

To better understand the culture of a people, it is important to know something about their background and how their everyday practices and special celebrations came to be. Two major influences on every culture are historical events and religion. This is definitely the case with Hispanic culture. When we speak of Hispanic culture, it is somewhat difficult to define since its origins come from many different Latin American influences. There are, however, some strong common characteristics that are evident among people of Hispanic origin. Many of the traditions celebrated by Hispanic people today have their roots in a blending of celebrations and observances practiced by their ancestors many years ago.

This book contains three sections: History of Mexico and Central America, The Calendar and Holidays, and Other Celebrations and Fiestas. Each section contains information and hands-on activities to recreate artifacts, crafts, and symbols significant to Hispanic life. This combination of activities will provide students with a varied picture of the wealth of influences found in Hispanic culture.

In the first section, students will learn some of the early history of Mexico and Central America (Belize, Guatemala, El Salvador, Honduras, Nicaragua, Costa Rica, and Panama). Then, students will complete several activities related to this area's early history.

In the second section, students will be introduced to many holidays observed on the Hispanic calendar. Read about unique days and ways certain holidays are celebrated. The fun crafts, activities, and songs in this book make many of the Hispanic celebrations come to life.

In the third section, students will look at other special events recognized in Hispanic culture, and explore traditional food and music. This section gives students a broad picture of the everyday fun and excitement that occurs during celebrations such as birthdays and weddings.

In *Celebrating Hispanic Culture,* read about key facts and people who influenced Hispanic culture. But more importantly, complete activities that allow students to experience it, as well! Open the pages of this book to explore the amazing, rich heritage and blending of ideas and traditions that make Hispanic culture one to be celebrated!

History of Mexico and Central America

Some of the traditions, beliefs, and practices that are part of Hispanic culture today come from the native people who once occupied the areas we now know as Mexico and Central America. Three of the most influential tribes were the Olmecs, the Mayans, and the Aztecs. There were other significant tribes; however, these three civilizations left many lasting influences.

Another significant group of people, the Spanish, came to this area and greatly affected the way the native people lived. Because the Spanish conquered and colonized much of Mexico and Central America, they had quite a lasting effect on this area. Read on to learn about some of the history of Mexico and Central America to better understand some of the early influences on Hispanic Culture.

This section contains:
• A map showing territories of the Olmec, Mayan, and Aztec civilizations
• Information about the daily life and history of the Olmecs, Mayans, and Aztecs
• Information about the Spanish conquest and influence on Mexico and Central America
• Related hands-on activities

OLMEC, MAYAN, AND AZTEC TERRITORIES

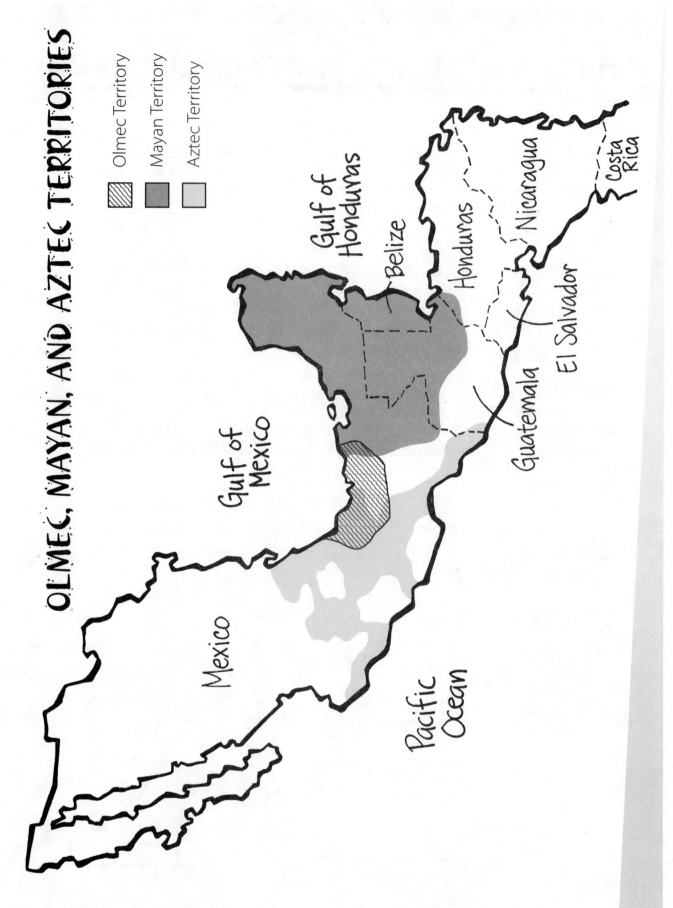

Olmec Territory

Mayan Territory

Aztec Territory

Gulf of Honduras

Belize

Honduras

Nicaragua

Costa Rica

El Salvador

Guatemala

Gulf of Mexico

Mexico

Pacific Ocean

Celebrating Hispanic Culture • CD-104040 • © Carson-Dellosa

THE OLMECS

1200 B.C. to 300 A.D.

Not much is known about the original inhabitants of what we know today as Mexico and Central America. The Olmecs were one of the earliest groups discovered. They are well-known for many contributions, including three religious centers. The Olmecs excelled in architecture, pottery, art, mathematics, and astronomy. Their skills in astronomy helped them to design a calendar that is almost as accurate as the one used today. The Olmecs mostly inhabited the areas of La Venta and San Lorenzo on the Gulf of Mexico.

Significant artifacts left behind by the Olmec civilization were huge sculpted stone heads. Some are as large as 8' (2.4 m) tall and weigh as much as 40 tons (36 metric tons). These huge pieces were carved and moved to the hilltops. Like the pyramids in Egypt, scientists do not know how the Olmecs moved the stones or why they were placed on the hilltops to overlook the land. The stones are sculpted into various combinations, mixing features of humans and animals, such as jaguars. Some have suggested that the stones were meant to be symbols of Olmec rulers.

THE MAYANS

300 A.D. to 900 A.D.

The Mayans were greatly influenced by the Olmecs, the advanced civilization that preceded them. Like the Olmecs, the Mayans, who inhabited present-day Yucatan Peninsula and Guatemala, carved out religious centers. Each of these areas centered around pyramids—large buildings constructed with square bases and triangular sides. The Mayans built Chichén Itzá and El Tajín in Vera Cruz.

Archeologists who have studied the Mayan civilization discovered many of their contributions to science and technology. These included observatories where Mayans studied the stars, which they used to design a yearly calendar. The Mayans are also known for their system of numbers and picture writing. They even had a road system, as well as rivers on which they traveled for trading, travel, and communication.

Those who study the Mayan civilization have also learned many interesting facts about the way Mayans lived. The priests were the most important people among the Mayans. They determined the laws regarding crime and taxation, and they oversaw construction and the planting and harvesting of crops.

Little is known about why the great Mayan empire lost its influence. Some speculate that the manner in which they harvested their crops contributed to the barren land. They used the strip-and-burn method of harvesting that eventually caused the soil to lose its fertility. This may have caused the Mayans to move from the city sites they occupied.

THE AZTECS

1200 A.D. to 1521 A.D.

The Aztecs, who lived in much of present-day Mexico, Guatemala, Honduras, El Salvador, and Belize, were another civilization that strongly influenced Hispanic culture. They were the last great tribe to inhabit this area before the Spanish came to conquer this portion of North and Central America.

Their belief in the Aztec sun god Huitzilopochtli strongly affected their lives. According to legend, the Aztecs left their land in Aztlan in search of a new home because they thought that Huitzilopochtli wanted them to move. They were to settle when they saw an eagle devouring a serpent while sitting on a cactus in the middle of a lake. The tribe wandered around pillaging other tribes until they came to Lake Texcoco. There, they saw a cactus, eagle, and snake on an island, so they built the magnificent city of Tenochtitlán.

In 1520 A.D., Hernando Cortez, a famous Spanish *conquistador* or conqueror, and his men landed off the shore of Mexico at a bay that he named Vera Cruz. He continued on into the heart of Mexico, looking for the city of Tenochtitlán, where the Aztecs were. Once there, he met Montezuma, the Aztec Indian chief. Montezuma had learned of Cortez's impending arrival through spies, but from the description of Cortez, the chief believed that Cortez was the legendary god Quetzalcoatl, who had returned with his band of immortal men. This belief eventually led to the downfall of the Aztec empire because Cortez and his men proved not to be gods, but Spanish who defeated the Aztecs and overtook their land, thus triggering the Spanish conquest of much of Mexico and Central America.

THE SPANISH

1520 A.D. to 1809 A.D.

Once the Spanish conquered the city of Tenochtitlán, they tore down the pyramids and worship centers and built directly on top of the Aztec ruins. They quickly settled the area as their own. The Spanish introduced their religion of Catholicism. Many native people combined Catholicism with their existing religious practices. Many priests came from Spain to further share Catholicism.

Another result of the Spanish conquest over Mexico and Central America was the racial mixing of native people and the Spanish. The Spanish conquistadors had not brought women with them, so when they settled in the area, they married the women from various native groups, resulting in many young *mestizos* (people of mixed Indian and European ancestry). The blending of these two peoples furthered the influence of the Spanish and caused a blending of cultures that is evident in Hispanic culture today.

The success of Cortez and his men led to further exploration by other Spanish. After silver was discovered in 1546 A.D., Spain wanted to maintain control over their newly acquired territory because they were interested in this new source of wealth. The silver brought even more people to what became known as "New Spain." These new Spanish colonists further developed much of the land. Many of these wealthy settlers built rather large ranches that contained sizable herds of cattle and sheep.

After many years of rule by Spain, the people began an independence movement on September 16, 1810. Father Miguel Hidalgo led the cry of revolt against Spanish rule in Mexico. (See page 38.) Even though Hidalgo was captured and killed a year later, another priest, José Maria Morelos, kept up the fight. Once they finally gained their independence from Spain, the people referred to their new country as the Republic of Mexico.

 Celebrating Hispanic Culture • CD-104040 • © Carson-Dellosa

Materials:

- Newspaper
- Newspaper strips, 2" x 12" (5 cm x 30.5 cm)
- Chicken wire (optional)
- Glue and water mixture (1:1 ratio) or liquid starch
- Craft paints
- Craft paintbrushes

Teacher Note:
*If making one very large stone head as a class, use chicken wire to form the stone head shape.

Olmec Stone Head

Much has been said about the amazing, huge stone heads made by the Olmecs. Create your own using the instructions below. Make a large one to represent the entire class or have each student design a small stone head for herself.

Procedure:

1. Form a large piece of newspaper into a rounded, head shape.*
2. Dip the newspaper strips into the starch or glue mixture and wrap them around the head shape. Allow this layer to dry before adding a new one.
3. Keep wrapping the newspaper strips until there is a shape of a large head.
4. Using newspaper, build up facial features, such as a nose, mouth, chin, and forehead.
5. Let it dry, then paint the head to represent yourself or another important figure.

Sun God

Most native groups worshipped at least one sun god, such as the Aztec god Huitzilopochtli. Below are instructions to make a representation of a sun god, a recognizable icon in Hispanic history.

Procedure:

1. Roll out a ball of salt dough to approximately 1" thickness onto a flat, floured surface.
2. Place a paper plate onto the flattened dough. Use a plastic knife to cut around the plate to form a circle. Set aside the extra dough.
3. Remove the plate and place the dough circle on a cookie sheet. This circular piece of dough forms the foundation for the face.
4. Using the extra dough, roll out another flat piece and a rope. Use the flat piece to cut out shapes, such as circles and triangles, to create facial features. Use the rope piece to form sun rays and any other unique features.
5. Add the dough features to the dough circle by gently pressing them in with wet fingers. Use a wooden craft stick to smooth and connect the dough pieces.
6. Use the tip of a toothpick to make a hole at the top for hanging.
7. Let an adult bake the dough face in an oven at 200°F (93°C) until it begins to brown slightly and harden (approximately five minutes).
8. When cooled, paint the face using bright colors. Hang the completed sun god face using sturdy yarn.

Materials:

- Salt dough (See below.)
- Rolling pin
- Paper plate
- Flour
- Cookie sheet
- Plastic knife
- Toothpick
- Wooden craft stick
- Craft paints
- Craft paintbrushes
- Colorful yarn

Salt Dough:

2 cups flour
2 cups salt
1 cup cornstarch
1 cup water

Place ingredients into a large bowl and mix by hand thoroughly until dough feels like clay.

Materials:

- Paper
- Pencil
- Salt dough
  (See page 12.)
- Toothpick
- Craft paint (optional)
- Craft paintbrushes
  (optional)

Teacher Note:
This activity can be completed individually or with small groups.

Mayan Statue

Not much is known about the average Mayan; however, there are records of the rulers and their achievements because of the statue columns that the Mayans left behind. These statues were large columns that contained etchings with information about the laws and rulers. The statue scribes often made the rulers seem mighty and added godly characteristics to the rulers' personalities. Each statue was not intended to be a likeness of the person, but was a symbol of his power.

Procedure:

1. Write down a list of symbols and their meanings to represent facts about yourself or culture.
2. Form the salt dough into the shape of a standing column.
3. Using a toothpick, scratch the symbols in the dough on all four sides of the dough pillar.
4. Let an adult bake the statue in an oven at 200° F (93° C) until it begins to brown slightly and harden (approximately eight minutes).
5. If desired, paint your column.

Costa Rican Cart

The Costa Rican cart (*carreta*) is a well-recognized, traditional symbol of Central America. Originally, these functional forms of transport toted large amounts of coffee. Later, families began to arrive to community fiestas in their fancy, painted *carretas* as they became status symbols.

Procedure:

1. Cover a working surface with newspaper. Paint the inside of the shoe box with white paint and let dry. Turn over the box, paint the outside white, and let dry.
2. On cardboard, trace around a CD to make four circles. Mark the center of each wheel. Use a pencil to poke a small slit in the center of the wheel for the brass fastener.
3. Paint one side of each wheel white. Let them dry. Then, paint the other side of the wheels white, and let them dry.
4. Paint the inside and outside of the cart using bright colors. Let it dry.
5. Paint designs on the cart and wheels.
6. Push the fasteners through the sides of the shoe box to attach the wheels to the cart. Be sure the wheels are even before making holes in the box.
7. Fill the cart with paper flowers (see directions on page 32) or other festive decorations.

Materials:

- Newspaper
- Shoe box
- Cardboard (enough to make four wheels for the cart)
- Promotional or other CD
- 4 brass fasteners
- White latex paint
- Craft paint in many bright colors
- Craft paintbrushes
- Pencil
- Scissors

Materials:

- Self-drying clay
- Rolling pin
- Plastic knife
- Bowl of water
- Craft paint (optional)
- Craft paintbrushes (optional)

Clay Bowl

The Mayan people made their pottery by hand because there were no potter's wheels. They used clay coils to form pots, or cut thin pieces of clay and shaped pots by hand. The red clay pots from Mexico today are made from red clay or clay mixed with natural dyes.

Procedure:

1. Roll out the clay onto a flat surface to about ¼" (0.64 cm) in thickness.
2. Cut the clay into a circular shape.
3. With additional clay, roll out long, thin ropes of clay.
4. Place the clay ropes around the outer edge of the circle and gradually coil up the ropes to form the sides of the bowl.
5. With wet fingers, smooth together the clay coils.
6. Form a lip around the top of the bowl by bending the top edge of the bowl between your index fingers. Then, let the bowl dry.
7. Roll out more clay onto a flat surface to about ¼" (0.64 cm) in thickness. Place the dried bowl (top down) on the flat clay. Cut around the top of the bowl to make a lid.
8. Use the leftover clay to make a handle on the lid. With wet fingers, smooth together the handle and lid. Dry the lid and bowl separately.
9. Paint designs on the dried bowl if desired.

Paper Figure

The Mayans are credited with having first made *amate* paper over 1,000 years ago. This paper is still used by some people today. To make it, bark is cut from an amate tree, and the bark is boiled to make it soft. Then, the softened bark is placed on a board and pounded with a stone until it is flat like paper. The *amate* paper has many uses in arts and crafts. It is often formed into special paper figures, and is used for beautiful, vibrant paintings. *Amate* paper is also folded and cut to make amulets to wear around the neck or hang on walls. Some believe the amulets help protect them from sickness or danger.

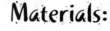

Materials:

- Large paper grocery bag
- Craft paint
- Craft paintbrushes
- Coarse brush
- Pencil
- Scissors

Procedure:

1. Tear the front section from a grocery bag, giving the paper a slightly rough edge.
2. Crumble the paper several times to make it worn and somewhat soft.
3. Spread out the paper and paint designs on it.
4. After it is dry, scrape the bag with a coarse brush to give it a primitive look.
5. To make a paper figure, fold the paper in half lengthwise.
6. On one side of the paper (including the folded area), draw a special design representing yourself or an object that you like.
7. Cut out the design. Cut the design on the fold so that the paper will stay together.

Materials:

- 2 balloons
- Dried beans
- Newspaper strips, 2" x 12" (5 cm x 30.5 cm)
- Glue and water mixture (1:1 ratio) or liquid starch
- Craft paint
- Craft paintbrushes

Teacher Note:
Caution: Before completing any balloon activity, ask families about possible latex allergies. Also, remember that uninflated or popped balloons may present a choking hazard.

Balloon Maracas

Festivals with music and dancing were vital parts of the Mayan and Aztec cultures. There were various celebrations each month, including festivals to celebrate the important farming seasons. These events often included the musical sounds made from dried gourds or conch shells filled with seeds. Today, in Mexico and Central America, dancers reenact the ancient dances, often using an updated form of the maracas.

Procedure:

1. Put several dried beans inside two uninflated balloons.
2. Inflate the balloons and tie them.
3. Cover the balloons with layers of newspaper strips dipped in the glue mixture or starch. Allow each layer to dry before adding a new one. Extend the newspaper strips out at the stem of each balloon to form a handle.
4. When the maracas are dry, paint them with colorful designs. When dry, shake them to make festive music.

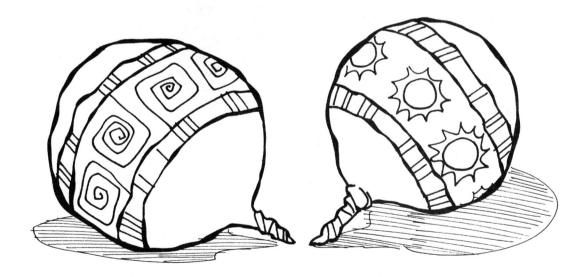

Egg Carton Maracas

Following is another variation of maracas using egg cartons.

Procedure:

1. Cut individual egg cups from the carton. It takes two cups to make each maraca. (A one dozen egg carton will make six maracas).
2. Add beans or pebbles to one cup.
3. Poke a hole in the bottom of the other cup. Insert a wooden craft stick or pencil and tape it in place to form a handle.
4. Tape the two cups together. Then, cover the cups with crepe paper strips dipped in the starch or glue mixture. Cover the handle so that it is firmly anchored to the maraca. Let it dry.
5. Decorate the maraca with painted designs.
6. Repeat steps 1-5 to make another maraca.

Materials:

- Cardboard egg carton
- Scissors
- Dried beans or pebbles
- Glue and water mixture (1:1 ratio) or liquid starch
- Crepe paper
- Wooden craft sticks or pencils
- Masking tape
- Craft paint
- Craft paintbrushes

Materials:

- 2 sheets of white paper, 8½" x 11" (21.5 cm x 28 cm)
- 2 pieces of white poster board, 5½" x 4¼" (14 cm x 11 cm)
- Markers
- Pencil
- Transparent tape
- Scissors

The Codex

The codex was used by both the Mayan and Aztec civilizations. It was like a foldout picture book written by a scribe. The codex recorded history, calendars, and information about the gods and the daily lives of the people. The scribes used glyphs, or picture symbols, to write the information.

Procedure:

1. Fold two sheets of paper in half lengthwise, then cut the paper on the folds.
2. Fold each strip of paper in half widthwise.
3. Join the short ends of the strips with transparent tape so that the strips make one long sheet.
4. Flip over the long sheet so that the tape is on the back.
5. Fold the pages into an accordion-pleated book.
6. Glue poster board to the front and back to make the book covers.
7. Decorate and fill your book with glyphs telling about a story or about yourself.

Aztec Shield

The Aztecs were known to challenge other tribes. During conflicts, the Aztec warriors often took their prisoners as slaves. The Aztec warriors were not paid; however, they did receive land, slaves, or clothing for their service. The warriors were easily recognized because they carried unique shields.

Materials:

- Cardboard
- Feathers
- Pencil
- Craft paints
- Craft paintbrushes
- Scissors
- Glue
- Brass fasteners

Procedure:

1. Cut a large circle from cardboard.
2. On the front, draw and paint a picture of a brave and fierce symbol, such as a jaguar or an eagle.
3. Glue feathers around the edge of the shield.
4. Form a handle on the back of the shield by attaching a strip of cardboard with brass fasteners.

Celebrating Hispanic Culture • CD-104040 • © Carson-Dellosa

Materials:

- Thick foam board
- Utility knife
- Green construction paper
- Red poster board
- Promotional or other CDs (optional)
- Wooden dowel
- Scissors
- Masking tape
- Glue
- Craft paints
- Craft paintbrushes
- Craft feathers
- Mixed colors of felt or construction paper
- Colorful yarn

Feather Fan

The Aztecs used feathers in their art, including their dance and music. They made other beautiful objects with feathers, and noblemen also used feathers in hot weather to fan themselves.

Procedure:

1. Draw two circles about 18" (46 cm) in diameter on the thick foam board. Then, draw two circles about 12" (30.5 cm) in the centers of the 18" (46 cm) circles. Have an adult use a utility knife to cut out the circles to make two large rings.
2. Cut out several leaf shapes from green paper and glue them around the outside edge the large foam ring. Then, glue craft feathers on top of the leaves on the outside edge of the ring. Cut shapes from colorful felt or paper and glue them to the other foam ring. Set aside to dry.
3. Cut two circles about 4¾" (12 cm) in diameter from red poster board. If desired, trace around a CD to make circles that are the correct size.
4. Paint a flower on one red circle and a butterfly on the other.
5. Tape pieces of yarn to the center back of one red circle. Place the first foam ring (leaf side up) over the red circle.
6. Tape the yarn to the foam ring to look like spokes. Tape the wooden dowel to the red circle. Coat the other ring with white glue and place it on top of the first, decorated side up.
7. Glue the second red circle on top of the first red circle, decorated side up.
8. Allow the completed fan to dry.

1.

2.

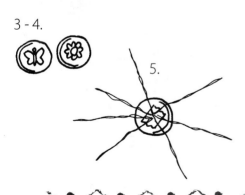

3 - 4.

5.

6 - 7.

8.

Mosaic Mask

In history and today, wearing a mask is a way that people can change the ordinary into the extraordinary. Masks were often used in tribal ceremonies. While wearing masks, people transformed their legends and myths into an entertaining art form. All individual personalities of the dancers or actors were lost and in their places stood the gods or other figures they represented. Not only were the dancers transformed, but the audience was transfixed by the ceremony. The following mask is made up of many small pieces of paper. However, the authentic tribal version would likely have been formed out of valuable stones.

Procedure:

1. Have an adult inflate a balloon to the same size as your head. Let him tie the balloon and cover it with petroleum jelly.
2. Dip newspaper strips into the starch or glue mixture and cover the front side of the balloon. Allow each layer to dry before adding a new one. Cover it with five layers of newspaper.
3. Using newspaper, build up facial features, such as a nose, mouth, chin, and forehead on the papier-mâché side of the balloon.
4. Once the papier-mâché is dry, have an adult carefully pop the balloon. Remove the mask and trim the sides.
5. Cover the mask with a light layer of glue, then add the various paper scraps. Make sure that the eyes and the mouth are recognizable with the paper scraps, too.
6. Share with others who or what the mask represents.

Materials:

- 1 balloon
- Petroleum jelly
- Newspaper strips, 2" x 12" (5 cm x 30.5 cm)
- Glue and water mixture (1:1 ratio) or liquid starch
- Bowl
- Scissors
- Scraps of colorful paper cut into various shapes
- Glue

Teacher Note:
Caution: Before completing any balloon activity, ask families about possible latex allergies. Also, remember that uninflated or popped balloons may present a choking hazard.

Materials:

- Half of a coconut shell (If not available, make papier-mâché half coconuts.)
- Craft paints
- Craft paintbrushes
- Colorful yarn
- Feathers
- Glue

Teacher Notes:
Ahead of time, drill a hole in a coconut and drain the milk. Cut the coconut in half. Share the meat with students.

Caution: Before completing any food activity, ask families' permission and inquire about students' food allergies and religious or other food preferences.

Coconut Mask

In some places, real coconut shells were used to make colorful masks. Complete the following directions to make a more authentic tribal mask replica.

Procedure:

1. Lay the flat, cut side of the coconut shell on a flat surface.
2. Paint designs on the shell to indicate facial features.
3. Decorate the shell with feathers and yarn to represent other features, such as hair and eyelashes. Let the mask dry.
4. Share with others who or what the mask represents.

Guatemalan Worry Doll

These handmade dolls are called worry dolls or trouble dolls because, originally, children took the dolls to bed with them and told the dolls their troubles so that they would have a good night's sleep. During the night, the doll was believed to do the worrying for the child.

Procedure:

1. Draw a face and hair on the top part of the clothespin and shoes on the bottom.
2. Glue each half of the craft stick to the side of the pin to form an arm. Secure the arms by wrapping masking tape around them and then let the doll dry.
3. Wrap yarn around the doll starting at the neck. Cover each arm with yarn, leaving some space uncovered for the hands. Then, wrap the yarn around the waist and down one leg and back up the leg.
4. Wind the yarn down and then up the other leg. Tie off the yarn at the back.

Materials:

- Wooden doll pin or straight clothespin (the type with no metal attachment)
- Wooden craft stick
- Small handsaw or kitchen shears
- Sandpaper
- Colorful yarn
- Scissors
- Markers
- Glue
- Masking tape

Teacher Note:
Cut the wooden craft stick in half to form the doll's arms. Sand any rough or splintered edges.

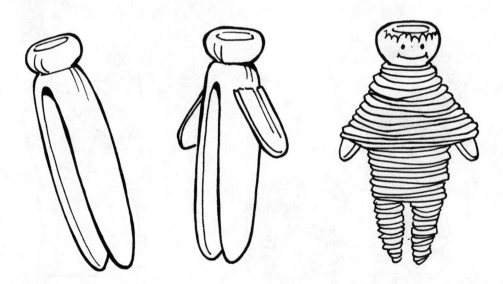

Materials:

- 3 twist ties, 3" (7.6 cm) long
- Colorful embroidery thread or thin yarn
- Scraps of colorful paper
- Scissors
- Glue
- Black fine-tipped marker

Miniature Worry Doll

The following instructions will create a small, simplified version of a worry doll using twist ties.

Procedure:

1. Hold two twist ties together and twist about 1" (2.5 cm) from the top.
2. Twist a third twist tie around the other two to make arms. Bend the ends to make hands and feet.
3. Knot a piece of thread or yarn to the twist ties where they cross and leave a piece of thread hanging.
4. Wind the thread around the waist and down one leg, then wind the thread back up the leg.
5. Wind the thread down and up the other leg. Knot the thread to the piece left hanging and trim the ends.
6. With a different color of thread, tie a knot around the waist and leave a piece of thread hanging. Wrap the chest and wrap down and up one arm and then the other. Crisscross the thread over the chest to finish and tie with the piece left hanging. Cut the ends and glue both knots to the doll.
7. Cut two small circles from paper scraps. Draw a face on one circle and hair on the other. Glue the circles together with the exposed twist tie between them.

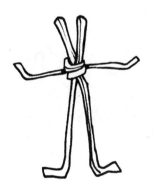

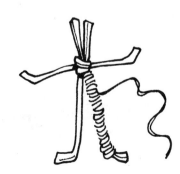

Woven Sash

Mexico and the countries of Central America, particularly Guatemala, are known for their clothes and blankets made up of vibrant and rich colors. Many of the fabrics are woven by hand, just as they have been for several hundreds of years. A traditional piece of woven clothing is a sash.

Materials:

- Four plastic drinking straws
- One skein of yarn
- Yarn needle
- Scissors
- Tape measure

Procedure:

1. Cut four pieces of yarn, 80" (203 cm) long.
2. Cut ½" (1.3 cm) off the end of each straw and keep the pieces.
3. Thread a piece of yarn through the straw and through the ½" (1.3 cm) piece of straw and then return the yarn through the straw. If needed, use a yarn needle to help get the yarn through the straw.
4. Repeat step 3 with the three additional straws.
5. Draw the ends of the yarn together and tie them in a tight knot.
6. Knot the end of the yarn on the skein to the end of one straw and weave it between each of the four straws, winding the yarn over one straw and under the next.
7. When you have woven about 3" (7.6 cm), push the yarn off the straws toward the knotted yarn.
8. Continue weaving until you run out of room to push the yarn. Cut off the yarn at the base of the pieces of straw and remove the straws.
9. Tie the remaining end of the sash into a tight knot. Leave yarn fringe at the ends of the sash. Trim as necessary.

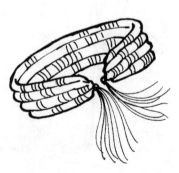

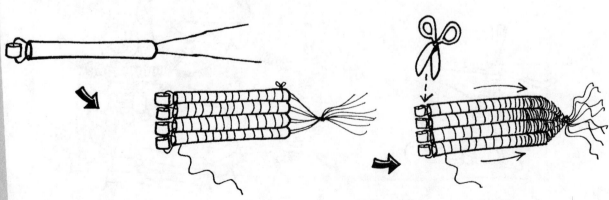

Materials:

- Pencil
- Ruler
- Piece of colorful construction paper, 12" x 18" (30.5 cm x 46 cm)
- 1" (2.5 cm) strips of various colors of construction paper (cut lengthwise)
- Scissors
- Glue
- Scraps of colorful yarn
- Hole punch
- Clear contact paper

Woven Place Mat

It is important to have a pretty table at *fiesta* or party time. Much attention is paid to detail to make celebrations festive and decorative, including the place settings. Tables are often set with fine place mats. Follow these instructions to continue the ancient weaving tradition.

Procedure:

1. Using a pencil and ruler, measure 1" (2.5 cm) around the border of a piece of brightly colored construction paper and draw lines to indicate it. (Black paper would also work.)
2. Measure and draw 1" (2.5 cm) lines from the top to the bottom borders.
3. Cut along the drawn lines, being careful not to cut through the borders of the paper.
4. Weave the paper strips one at a time, alternating direction. The first strip should be over a slit and then under to the end of the paper. The second strip should go under and then over to the end of the paper.
5. Glue the ends of the paper strips all on the same side of the paper. Let dry.
6. Cover the top and bottom of the place mat with clear contact paper.
7. Punch a hole in each corner of the place mat. Then, tie scraps of yarn through the holes to form tassels.

1.

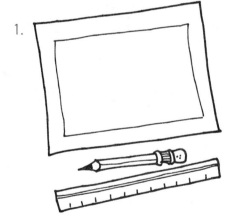

2 - 3.

4 - 7.

The next page contains a blank calendar reproducible. Hispanic cultures assign different saints to days of the year. Hispanic children are often given the names of the saints who share the dates of their births. Label a copy of the calendar reproducible with the current month and days. The months in Spanish are January/enero, February/febrero, March/marzo, April/abril, May/mayo, June/junio, July/julio, August/agosto, September/septiembre, October/octubre, November/noviembre, and December/diciembre. Also include Spanish holidays (listed below) on the appropriate days. Give each student a copy of the completed calendar. Have each student with a birthday that month research the saint associated with her birthday. (There are often multiple saints acknowledged for each day; have each student choose one saint to research.) Allow each birthday student to present information about her saint on her birthday. Encourage other students to record the student's birthday and the saint's name on the correct day on the calendar.

The remaining pages in this section are in chronological order to follow the Hispanic calendar. They are filled with information and activities to celebrate some of the many holidays recognized in Hispanic culture. Some of the holidays mentioned are celebrated in specific areas of Mexico and Central America, while most of them are acknowledged by Hispanic people throughout the world. Many of the holidays are followed by hands-on activities. The Day of the Dead and Christmas celebrations contain numerous activities because these two holidays are often the most highly anticipated events each year.

This section contains information about the following holidays:
St. Anthony's Day—January 17
The Virgin of Masaya Celebration—March 16
The San José Fair—March 19
Carnival—February or March, beginning the day before Lent
Holy Week—the week before Easter
Cinco de Mayo—May 5
The Day of Corpus Christi—occurring in June around the summer solstice
The Day of John the Baptist—June 24
Independence Day—September 16/September 15
Day of the Race—October 12/September 18
The Day of the Dead—November 1-2
The Day of the Virgin of Guadalupe—December 12
Christmas Celebrations—December 16-January 6
The Day of Innocents—December 28

LUNES	MARTES	MIÉRCOLES	JUEVES	VIERNES	SÁBADO	DOMINGO

ST. ANTHONY'S DAY

On January 17, St. Anthony's Day is celebrated with the blessing of the animals. Many people decorate their pets or their farm animals with flowers or other decorations. They then take their animals to church to be blessed by a priest.

THE VIRGIN OF MASAYA CELEBRATION

Masaya is a small town nestled in the shadow of a volcano in Nicaragua. On March 16, 1772, many believe that a miracle occurred when the volcano erupted and threatened the town. The tradition holds that the priest grabbed the statue of the Virgin Mary and ran up and down the streets of Masaya praying. The story goes on to say that the sky became dark and cloudy and it began to rain, which extinguished the fires in the volcano. Every year, the town celebrates the miracle with a special procession. Early in the morning of March 16, women dress the statue of the Virgin Mary with flowers. People then parade in front of the statue and touch it to receive blessings. When all have passed by, the statue is then veiled and put on a large board, and it is carried throughout the town much in the same way it was by the priest in 1772. The entire town joins in the parade.

Celebrating Hispanic Culture • CD-104040 • © Carson-Dellosa

THE SAN JOSÉ FAIR

Prior to 900 B.C., Copán was known as a great, flourishing Mayan city. However, around 900 A.D., the city suddenly disappeared, leaving only the ruins which were hidden within the jungle for many years. Today, there is a city very close to the Guatemalan border in Honduras near the Mayan ruins of Copán named Copán Ruinas. The citizens of Copán Ruinas are very proud of their ancestry, and they have mixed Mayan and Spanish customs into a celebration for their patron saint, San José. For five days, the city plaza is filled with food and crafts, while the evenings are filled with dancing and music. The *piñata* entertains the children. On the morning of March 19 (the Catholic Day of San José), the villagers meet in front of the church for mass followed by a procession of people carrying the statue of San José. San José is usually dressed in a black cape and a straw hat. The day ends with dramatizations based on Mayan rituals.

CARNIVAL

Carnival begins the day before Lent, which is also known as the Christian Shrove Tuesday, Fat Tuesday, or Mardi Gras. (Lent is the 40 days between Ash Wednesday and Easter.) In many cultures, Lent is a time when a person gives up doing something he likes, such as eating chocolate. Carnival is just the opposite. It is a time of great celebration, fun, and sometimes mischief. Some stories say that the early Mexicans wore costumes and masks during Carnival to make fun of the Spanish. During the fun-filled time of Carnival, people throw flowers at others, and the children try to crack eggs filled with confetti on the heads of those passing by.

Party Flowers

Carnival is a time with a fun, party-like atmosphere and much decoration and adornment. Follow these instructions to make beautiful Carnival flowers. Once complete, the flowers can be tossed around in celebration of the start of this festive time.

Materials:

- 5 sheets of colorful tissue paper
- Chenille craft sticks or twist ties
- Scissors

Procedure:

1. Cut the tissue paper into 5" x 5" (13 cm x 13 cm) squares.
2. Stack five tissue paper squares on top of each other.
3. Gather the squares together in the center and join them by wrapping them together with a chenille craft stick or a twist tie.
4. Fluff the paper into the shape of a flower blossom.
5. Finish by trimming the edges of the paper to create a recognizable or unique flower design.

Materials:

- Raw egg
- Small bowl
- Sewing needle
- Tissue paper cut into confetti size or packages of precut confetti
- Tissue paper strips, 1" x 4" (2.5 cm x 10 cm)
- Glue
- Craft paintbrushes
- Masking tape

Teacher Note:
Caution: Raw or lightly cooked eggs may be contaminated with salmonella, a bacteria responsible for food poisoning. To prevent illness from bacteria, use only properly refrigerated, clean, sound-shelled, fresh, grade AA or A eggs; cook eggs until yolks are firm; and cook foods containing eggs thoroughly.

Eggshells with Confetti

Make your own confetti-filled eggs to add a special, fun surprise at Carnival.

Procedure:

1. Have an adult wash and dry a raw egg.
2. Have an adult use a needle to gently pierce the clean egg at both ends, making sure one hole is larger than the other.
3. Have an adult blow through the smaller hole, pushing the egg yolk and egg white through the other end into a bowl. Wash out the inside and outside of the egg.
4. Let the egg dry thoroughly.
5. When dry, fill the egg with the confetti and seal the hole with a small piece of masking tape.
6. Cover the egg with a tissue paper strip and gently brush with glue until the egg is covered. Continue to layer the paper strips and glue until the egg is covered.
7. Let the egg dry.

HOLY WEEK

In Christian churches, Holy Week (*Semana Santa*) happens the week before Easter. It is very important in most Hispanic households. Many of the stores in Hispanic countries close during this time, especially from Maundy Thursday (the Thursday of Holy Week) until Easter.

In some places, such as in El Salvador, people often craft special carpets on Maundy Thursday to cover the main streets for the procession that takes place on Good Friday. The carpets are made using sawdust, flowers, and dirt mixed with colorful dyes to create designs and pictures. For the procession, the people dress in costumes to reenact the journey of Jesus to the crucifixion. The procession includes people playing the roles of Roman soldiers and a giant figure of Christ that is carried on the shoulders of a team of men.

Materials:

- Construction paper
- Pencil
- Dark-colored yarn
- Colorful sand
- Small artificial flowers
- Other small, light objects, such as pebbles, that will adhere with glue
- Glue

Sand-Painted Carpets

Make your own painted "carpets" for Holy Week to recreate the special street procession.

Procedure:

1. Draw a simple design on a piece of construction paper.
2. Glue yarn over the outline.
3. Spread a thin layer of glue within the different sections created by the yarn.
4. Sprinkle sand into the sections to cover the glue.
5. Add flowers, small pebbles, or other small decorative objects to enhance the sand-painted piece.

CINCO DE MAYO

After Mexico won its independence, a new government had to be formed. Mexico found this to be a major challenge because it had been ruled by Spain for many years and the people had little experience in self-governing. At first, soldiers tried ruling, and then powerful groups fought amongst themselves to take over. The various governments that ruled were rather weak. Eventually, a war broke out between the United States and Mexico over the boundary line between the two countries. The United States won and Mexico lost a great deal of its land, which included the current states of California, Nevada, Utah, Arizona, and New Mexico.

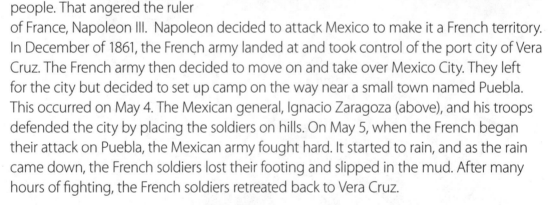

The Mexican government owed money to other countries, especially to France. Benito Juarez, the ruler at that time, had a choice: to use the treasury money to pay back France or to use the money to help the people of Mexico. He chose to help his people. That angered the ruler of France, Napoleon III. Napoleon decided to attack Mexico to make it a French territory. In December of 1861, the French army landed at and took control of the port city of Vera Cruz. The French army then decided to move on and take over Mexico City. They left for the city but decided to set up camp on the way near a small town named Puebla. This occurred on May 4. The Mexican general, Ignacio Zaragoza (above), and his troops defended the city by placing the soldiers on hills. On May 5, when the French began their attack on Puebla, the Mexican army fought hard. It started to rain, and as the rain came down, the French soldiers lost their footing and slipped in the mud. After many hours of fighting, the French soldiers retreated back to Vera Cruz.

A year later, the French tried again to take over, and this time they succeeded. They took control of Mexico City and placed Maximilian on the throne as ruler. The Battle of Puebla that had taken place the year before gave the Mexican soldiers the courage to try again. In 1867, the Mexican people overthrew Maximilian from power and forced Napoleon III to remove the French troops from Mexico. Now, each year on May 5, the people of Mexico acknowledge their amazing defeat over the French.

THE DAY OF CORPUS CHRISTI

The Day of Corpus Christi takes place in the month of June around the time of the summer solstice. In the Catholic church, this day is a commemoration of the Eucharist. This special day is well-known for the gift of mule toys. The mules are presented in different ways, such as a pair of small, mule-shaped earrings or even a life-size mule toy for a child to "ride." The legend surrounding this event says that when the early inhabitants of Mexico came to pay their dues to the church, they would often leave their mules tied up outside. The giving of mules today serves as a reminder of this custom.

Also on this day, an amazing dance is performed. It was originally done to pay tribute to and appease a sun god. It begins with five men climbing a tall pole, sometimes as tall as 1,000' (305 m). One man stays at the top of the pole, plays a small flute, and beats a drum while the other four men tie ropes around their waists and act as fliers. The ropes that are tied to the men have been wound around the pole so that when they let go, they unwind the ropes and must fly 13 revolutions from the top to the bottom.

THE DAY OF JOHN THE BAPTIST

On June 24, the Day of John the Baptist (*San Juan Bautista*) is celebrated. According to the Christian faith, John the Baptist baptized Jesus. People remember him by playing water games and activities. People take part in fun, summer merriment, such as sprinkling each other with water and having swimming parties.

INDEPENDENCE DAY

The Mexican Independence Day is a celebration much like that of the Fourth of July in the United States. This observance, which occurs on September 16, acknowledges Mexico's freedom from the Spanish, who arrived in 1521 and dominated Mexico for 500 years. While each Hispanic country has its own Independence Day, Mexico has a celebration to acknowledge its freedom. Incidentally, Costa Rica, El Salvador, Guatemala, Honduras, and Nicaragua all celebrate their independence on September 15.

Mexican independence became a reality with the help of Miguel Hildalgo. In 1753, Miguel Hidalgo was born in a little town north of Mexico City. He became a Catholic priest. He studied democracy and freedom. He grew to believe that Mexico should be free to govern itself. He was sent to a small village named Dolores where the people were very poor. They lived on wealthy estates owned by the Spanish colonists and worked very hard for their small wages. Father Hidalgo tried to educate them, but the wealthy landowners were opposed to his helping. He decided that the only way to make changes to better the lives of these oppressed people was to overthrow the government. On September 16, 1810, Father Hidalgo began ringing the church bells, calling the people to rise up against the Spanish rule. He is quoted as having said, "Long live our Lady Guadalupe! Down with the bad government! Death to the Spanish!" This call for freedom was known as the *Grito de Dolores*. Mexicans united, and thousands joined the crusade for freedom. Father Hidalgo himself was defeated and killed in 1811. However, he had left the Mexican people full of hope, and they continued to fight until 1821, when Mexico won its independence. For this reason, Father Hidalgo is called the Father of Independence. The church bells are rung each year on September 16, and the people repeat the *Grito de Dolores*. Also on this day, the President of Mexico steps onto the balcony in the National Palace and yells, "¡Viva México!" and "¡Viva la independencia!" And the people cheer back. The Mexican Independence Day celebration is highlighted with confetti and fireworks in red, white, and green (the colors of the Mexican flag).

Celebrating Hispanic Culture • CD-104040 • © Carson-Dellosa

DAY OF THE RACE

Every year on October 12, the United States celebrates Christopher Columbus's discovery of North America in 1492. In Mexico, they also have a special observance on this date called Day of the Race (*Día de la Raza)*, which celebrates the mixture of the Spanish blood with the blood of native Mexicans, creating *mestizos*. This mixing of peoples occurred as a result of Columbus's arrival to this new land.

In Puerta Limon, Costa Rica, celebrations are held on September 18 because it was on that date in 1502 that Christopher Columbus landed there. Apparently, when he saw many of the natives wearing jewelry and ornaments of gold, legend says that Columbus named the area Costa Rica because of the "rich coast."

THE DAY OF THE DEAD

According to ancient Hispanic belief, death was a release from daily suffering or strife and not to be feared. Many believed that the dead made a long and dangerous trip through eight underworlds before reaching the land of the dead. How the dead person was received there depended on his occupation and how his life on Earth ended.

When the Spanish came to North America and spread Christianity, they brought to the native people a new concept of death that involved the idea of good or bad and heaven or hell. The Spanish realized that the spiritual rituals of the natives were old and well-established and could not likely be changed, so as they shared Catholicism with the native people, the ancient celebrations of the dead continued. This mixing of beliefs and traditions is known today as folk Catholicism. The Day of the Dead is a perfect example of the blending of beliefs in Hispanic culture.

In Catholic tradition, the evening of October 31 was known as All Hallows' Eve (which was later referred to as Halloween). All Saints' Day is November 1, which is to commemorate the saints. November 2 is All Souls' Day, when people pray for all of the saints that have died. In Hispanic culture, there is a blended celebration on November 1 and 2, which is called *El día de los muertos* (The Day of the Dead). According to Hispanic tradition, the dead are given permission to come back to Earth to visit their friends and relatives to be sure that all is well and that they have not been forgotten. November 1 is to honor children, and November 2 is to honor adults. The celebrations have become more like a *fiesta* (party) rather than a holy day. The Day of the Dead is a major holiday in Hispanic countries and is planned for many months prior to the actual celebration. There is much to do to prepare for this special celebration. Skeletons appear in the form of toys and decorations, special breads are baked, an altar is set up to commemorate each dead person, banners of finely cut paper are hung, and flowers are placed everywhere.

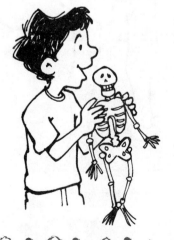

The Altar

The setting up of altars is a central part of the Day of the Dead. This custom is maintained to ensure good relations between those still alive and family members and friends who have died. A family works together to create a place to hold special things of the person who has died. On the altar where the offerings (or *ofrendas*) are placed, items that represent what the dead person enjoyed in life are included. The foods that the deceased enjoyed in life are prepared and placed on the altar along with pictures and flowers. Religious items are also included, mainly to ensure a safe passage back to the land of the dead. Incense is burned to complete the altar.

According to the Day of the Dead tradition, the dead wish for the things that they had in life, such as beautiful flowers, delicious food, and fun fireworks. In each town, there is a great *fiesta* (party) that begins with the cleaning of the tombstones, weeding and beautifying the graves, and covering the graves with flowers, pictures, and other special tokens to welcome the souls back to Earth.

As is the custom, a huge feast is held, and everyone celebrates with candies and foods, such as breads shaped like skeletons. In Santiago, Guatemala, the people get up very early to decorate every door with marigolds and to decorate the altars and the grave sites. They have the additional tradition of building huge kites and flying them on All Saints' Day and All Souls' Day. A big bonfire is held at sunset on November 2, and all of the kites are burned.

Flowers

The most commonly seen flowers (*flores*) during the Day of the Dead celebrations are marigolds because they are recognized as the flowers of the dead. These flowers are placed all over the towns, including on people's front doors.

Procedure:

1. Roll out several small, flat, thin pieces of yellow molding clay, approximately ½" (1.3 cm) thick, onto a flat surface.
2. Cut each clay piece into the shape of a marigold petal.
3. Form the center of the marigold with another thin piece of yellow molding clay.
4. Gather the center and the outside petals to form the flower.
5. Roll a thick strip of green molding clay to form a long stem.
6. Attach the stem to the flower by gently pressing the flower to the top of the stem.
7. Bake according to molding clay package directions.

Materials:

- Tissue paper
- Scissors
- String
- Stapler

Student Note:
To make the best banner, practice by completing the procedure using newspapers. Be sure to turn the paper when cutting and not the scissors.

Cut Paper Banners

Tissue paper is used to make these festive banners. This art form originally came from China and is often referred to as *papel de China*.

Procedure:

1. Fold the top edge of the tissue paper down 1" (2.5 cm) as the area to put the string for hanging. Do not cut this part.
2. Fold the paper in half vertically with the flap on the outside and fold again two more times, making sure that the edges are even.
3. Use the scissors to cut a decorative edge on the bottom.
4. Cut a design along the folded edges.
5. Carefully unfold the banner leaving the flap folded.
6. When a few banners have been made and are ready to be hung, place them on a flat surface. Place a long piece of string in the flap and staple the string together with the banner to prevent the paper from slipping.

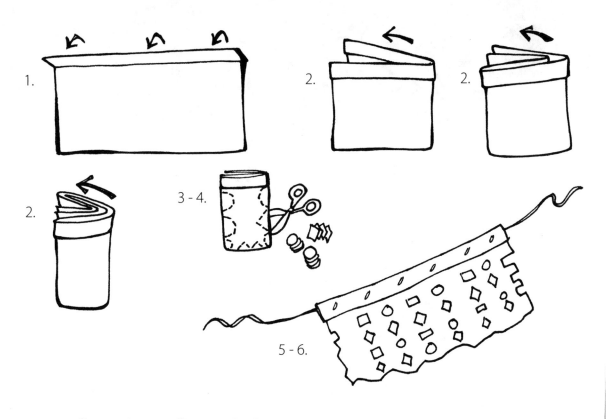

Skeletons

Skeletons are a significant part of the Day of the Dead celebration. They appear as toys and in the form of breads and candies. In addition, they are used in the dramas and music performed during this time. The skeleton has long been a part of Hispanic culture, not only as a symbol of death, but also to represent the continuity of life through the bones of the skeleton.

Skeleton toys are more than just fun trinkets for children. The toys are meant to teach the young about death, which helps them learn not to fear it but to accept it.

The early images used for skeletons during the Day of the Dead celebrations were rather straightforward. However, Mexican lithographer, José Guadalupe Posada (1852-1913), replaced the traditional skeleton with a more personalized caricature form called a *calaca*, which showed the skeleton likenesses acting out everyday activities.

Materials:

- Paper plate
- Pencil
- Scissors
- White paper
- Black felt-tipped pen
- Glue
- Hole punch
- Two 18" (46 cm) pieces of string

Paper Plate Skull Masks

Silly skull masks are a fun way for students to get in a festive mood for The Day of the Dead.

Procedure:

1. Hold a paper plate close to a partner's face, with the eating surface toward the face. Gently mark the location of the eyes and nose with a pencil. Return the plate to your partner and have her repeat step 1 with you, using a different plate.
2. Cut holes where the eyes and nose are marked and outline them heavily with a black felt-tipped pen.
3. Cut one 1½" x 4" (3.8 cm x 10 cm) strip of paper from the white paper. Draw teeth on the paper strip leaving ½" (1.3 cm) blank on each end.
4. For the mouth, glue both ends of the paper strip (step 3) to the plate so that the teeth protrude.
5. Punch holes on the sides of the plate. Place the string through the holes and pull them through. Tie the strings to the plate and then around your head.

Skull Mobile

Another decoration perfect for a Day of the Dead celebration is a skull mobile.

Procedure:

1. Trace the skull pattern on a square of white poster board. Draw the skull features on the poster board using the pattern as a guide.
2. Outline the eyes, nose, and mouth heavily with a black felt-tipped pen.
3. Decorate the skull and color it.
4. Repeat the design on the other side of the skull.
5. Punch a hole at the top of the skull and tie a piece of string to the hole, then tie it to a coat hanger.
6. Repeat steps 1-5 to make additional skulls to complete the mobile.

Materials:

- Skull pattern (page 47)
- Several 3" x 3" (7.6 cm x 7.6 cm) squares of white poster board
- Pencil
- Black felt-tipped pen
- Markers or crayons
- Scissors
- Hole punch
- String
- Metal coat hanger

Celebrating Hispanic Culture • CD-104040 • © Carson-Dellosa

Skull Patterns

Dancing Skeleton Puppet

This interactive toy will make students laugh as they create these dancing puppet toys.

Procedure:

1. Color the skeleton puppet pattern.
2. Cut apart the puppet pieces.
3. Attach the brass fasteners through the X marks to hold the puppet pieces together.
4. Glue the guitar to the hands of the skeleton.
5. Glue the dowel to the back of the body of the skeleton. Allow it to dry.
6. Pull a piece of string through the part of the arm marked with an A and tie a knot.
7. To make the skeleton dance, pull the string gently as you hold the skeleton by the dowel.

Materials:

- Copy of skeleton puppet pattern on sturdy paper (page 49)
- Pencil
- Scissors
- Brass fasteners
- Glue
- Crayons
- String
- Wooden dowel

Skeleton Puppet Patterns

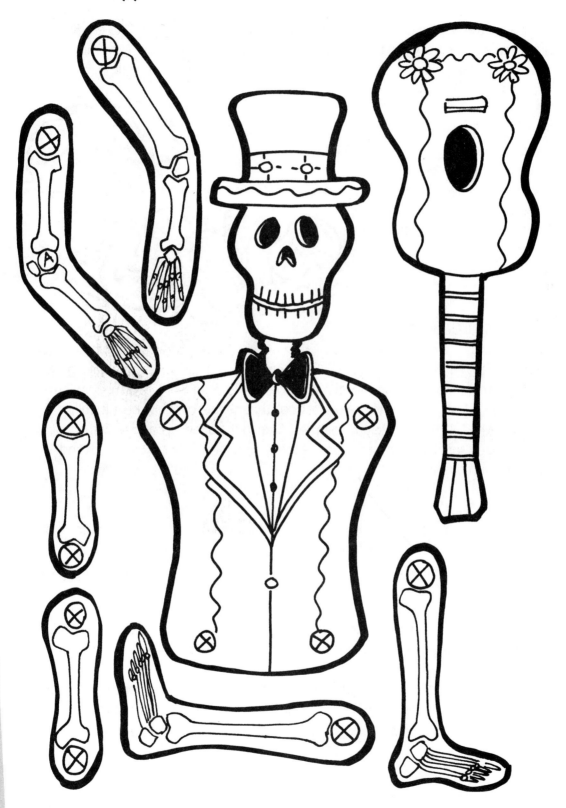

Sugar Skull Cookies

The Day of the Dead would not be complete without something good to eat. Sugar skull cookies are brought to the local markets about one week before November 2. Thousands of skull cookies are sold. They are traditionally made out of almond paste, refined sugar, egg whites, and lime juice.

INGREDIENTS:
2 cups almonds
2½ cups confectioners' sugar
2 small egg whites, beaten lightly
½ teaspoon almond extract
1 container of prepared frosting

ALMOND SKULL COOKIES:
Place almonds in a medium saucepan. Cover with water and cook for 10 minutes over medium heat. Allow to cool and remove almond skins. Dry almonds on a baking rack for 10 minutes. Grind them in a food processor with the sugar until the mixture forms a thick paste. Add egg whites to the paste. Cook the mixture over low heat to fully cook the eggs whites (approximately 10 minutes). Spread the almond paste on wax paper that has been sprinkled with sugar. Shape the dough into several skull shapes and decorate with frosting.

EASY SKULL COOKIES:
Using refrigerated cookie dough, form each cookie into skull shape using approximately a tablespoon of dough. Bake according to package directions, then decorate each cookie with prepared frosting.

Teacher Notes:
Caution: Before completing any food activity, ask families' permission and inquire about students' food allergies and religious or other food preferences.

Caution: Raw or lightly cooked eggs may be contaminated with salmonella, a bacteria responsible for food poisoning. To prevent illness from bacteria, use only properly refrigerated, clean, sound-shelled, fresh, grade AA or A eggs; cook eggs until yolks are firm; and cook foods containing eggs thoroughly.

Bread of the Dead

These small loaves of bread represent the souls of the departed. The Bread of the Dead or *pan de muerto* is made to please the appetites of the living; however, the loaves are often placed on the altars for the dead.

INGREDIENTS:

3½ cups flour	½ cup sugar
1 teaspoon salt	1 tablespoon anise seed
2 packages dry yeast	½ cup warm milk
½ cup water	½ cup margarine
4 eggs	

Mix the dry ingredients (including just 1½ cups of flour). Add warm milk, water, margarine, and mix together. Add the eggs and remaining flour and mix together. Knead on a lightly floured board for 8-10 minutes. Place dough into a greased bowl and let it rise until it has doubled (1½ hours). Punch down the dough and form into oval shapes. Let the dough rise again for 1 hour. Bake the loaves at 350°F (177°C) for 40 minutes. As they cool, cover each loaf with glaze. (See below.)

GLAZE:
½ cup sugar
⅓ cup orange juice
2 tablespoons grated orange peel

Boil sugar, orange juice, and orange peel for 2 minutes and brush onto the warm bread.

Teacher Notes:
Caution: Before completing any food activity, ask families' permission and inquire about students' food allergies and religious or other food preferences.

Caution: Raw or lightly cooked eggs may be contaminated with salmonella, a bacteria responsible for food poisoning. To prevent illness from bacteria, use only properly refrigerated, clean, sound-shelled, fresh, grade AA or A eggs; cook eggs until yolks are firm; and cook foods containing eggs thoroughly.

The Dance of the Old Men

Dancing is a common element in many Hispanic celebrations. The following dance is done during the many Day of the Dead activities. Called the Dance of the Old Men (*La danza de los viejitos*), it is performed by young men who represent old men. The dancers exaggerate the hobble and posture of the elderly. The dancers look as if it is very painful to walk; they hold their backs while stooping over. They begin the dance slowly and sluggishly. The accompanying music is usually performed on guitar.

Each *viejito* is traditionally dressed in white pants, a mask, a bright kerchief, a sombrero, a cotton shirt, a serape (a woven poncho), and black or brown shoes with taps. Each dancer also has white stringy hair and holds a cane.

SHORTENED VERSION OF THE DANCE
The dance has three parts. The first part is performed very slowly but still rhythmically. The second part becomes livelier, and the dancers jump and leap about with vigor for about one minute. Then, the third part is a repetition of the first, where the dancers return to a slow, unathletic gait.

DANCE MOVEMENTS

Right heel on floor (tap twice)
Right toe on floor (tap twice)
Left heel on floor (tap twice)
Left toe on floor (tap twice)
Step right foot across left foot (tap three times)
Step left foot across right foot (tap three times)
Cane on floor (tap five times)
Twist head right (hold for 3 counts)
Twist head left (hold for 3 counts)
Twist torso right (hold for 3 counts)
Twist torso left (hold for 3 counts)
Cane on floor (tap five times)
Jump forward, feet together (hold for 3 counts)
Jump backward, feet together (hold for 3 counts)

Materials:

- Pencil
- White paper plates
- Scissors
- Markers
- Two 18" (46 cm) pieces of string
- Hole punch
- White yarn
- Craft paint
- Craft paintbrushes
- Glue
- Cotton balls

Masks for the Dance

To make the Dance of the Old Men complete, students can design their own masks to take on the appearance of the *viejitos*.

Procedure:

1. Hold a paper plate close to a partner's face, with the eating surface toward the face. Gently mark the location of eyes, nostrils, and mouth with a pencil. Return the plate to your partner and have him repeat step 1 with you.
2. Cut out holes for the eyes, nostrils, and mouth.
3. Paint the mask to look like an old man's face.
4. Punch a hole on each side of the plate and attach a piece of yarn on each side.
5. Make several more small holes on each side and at the top of the mask. Tie pieces of white yarn onto the plate to represent hair.
6. Glue cotton balls above the eye holes for eyebrows.

THE DAY OF THE VIRGIN DE GUADALUPE

Legend says that on December 9, 1531, Juan Diego, a peasant and new convert to Christianity, saw a brown-skinned apparition of the Virgin Mary. The vision took place on a hill in Tepeyac, a village close to Mexico City that was dedicated to the Aztec mother goddess, Tonantzin.

According to the story, Mary told Juan Diego to go to the archbishop and tell him to build a church on that site. When Juan Diego told the archbishop of the plans, he scoffed at the peasant. On December 12, Juan Diego went back to the place where he had the vision, and Mary reappeared to him. At this encounter, Mary told Juan Diego to take some fresh roses from Tepeyac to give to the archbishop. Ordinarily, no roses grew on the dry, stony ground, and for them to bloom in December was indeed miraculous. When Juan Diego found the roses, he carefully picked them, placed them in his cloak, and took them back to the archbishop's palace. When Diego opened his cloak to drop the roses, everyone around saw the image of the Virgin Mary etched into his cloak. This event hastened the acceptance of Christianity in the region, since the people believed that the Virgin Mary must care for them a great deal, having come to them as an equal with brown skin like their own. By 1746, the Virgin of Guadalupe was chosen as the patron of all of New Spain from Upper California to Guatemala and San Salvador.

On December 12, many people come to Guadalupe to celebrate the amazing event. On this day, people gather to thank the Virgin Mary for answering their prayers. There are also *concero* dancers, dressed much like the ancient Aztec dancers, who wear shells around their ankles that make unique music while they dance.

Celebrating Hispanic Culture • CD-104040 • © Carson-Dellosa

Materials:

- 12" (30.5 cm) red crepe paper
- Florist tape
- Pencil
- Scissors
- Green chenille craft stick
- Green construction paper

Roses for the Virgin Mary

Create simple, beautiful roses following these instructions.

Procedure:

1. Roll a strip of red crepe paper into itself and gather it at one end.
2. Use a piece of florist tape to hold the gathered end.
3. At the top of the gathered crepe paper, cut various rounded edges.
4. Gently pull each cut edge to indicate varied rose petals.
5. Use another piece of florist tape to attach a green chenille craft stick to make a flower stem.
6. Cut leaves from green construction paper. Use florist tape to attach two or three leaves near the top of the stem.

CHRISTMAS CELEBRATIONS

The Christmas holidays in Hispanic homes are an ongoing celebration. Beginning with *Las Posadas* on December 16, followed by Christmas Eve on December 24, then Christmas Day (*La Navidad*) on December 25. The holidays are concluded on January 6 with the Day of the Kings (El *Día de los Reyes*). *Las Posadas* (which means inn or lodging) is a tradition that finds its origin at a convent near Tenochtitlán, where Fray Diego de Soria received permission from the Pope in Rome to celebrate the nine masses of gift giving, *Misas de Aguinaldo*. The masses were to be celebrated outdoors from December 16 through December 24 to correlate with the nine-day journey of Mary and Joseph from Nazareth to Bethlehem just before the birth of Christ.

Today, *Las Posadas* is a joyous Christmastime festivity in many Hispanic communities with many nights of celebrations as people reenact the journey of Mary and Joseph. It begins with people divided into two groups—those in the procession asking for lodging and those in the houses refusing the lodging. Mary and Joseph, the angels, and the shepherds carry candles and the nativity scene (*nacimiento*). They knock on a door and sing a special song, making a request to enter. The innkeepers respond with the traditional passages denying them entry. Mary and Joseph finally find lodging, and everyone gathers together and sings. *Piñatas* are broken, spilling with treats, then food and drink is shared. The festivities continue well into the night.

The nativity scene is a very significant part of the Christmas holidays. It consists of figurines of Mary, Joseph, the crèche (representation of baby Jesus in the manger), the animals, the shepherds, the angels, and the three wise men or magi. On Christmas Eve, a special mass is held at midnight. After the service, the baby Jesus figurine is placed in the manger. On Christmas Day, the wise men begin their journey to the nativity scene. Each day, the wise men figurines are moved closer to the nativity scene until the Day of the Kings arrives. That evening, the children put pairs of shoes outside the front doors with sweets for the magi or kings and straw for their camels. If a child has been good, the kings will leave the shoes filled with toys and candy. After January 6, the nativity scene is carefully packed away for another year. Many households take care to place the angel on the top, believing it will bless them and provide good fortune in the year to come.

Materials:

- Paper plate
- Markers or crayons
- Scissors
- Transparent tape
- Glue
- Ribbon

Gifts

Gifts called *aguinaldos* are exchanged at Christmastime. These special little gifts are shared during *Las Posadas* and other similar celebrations.

Procedure:

1. Cut a paper plate in half. (This will make two *aguinaldos*.)
2. Draw designs on both halves.
3. Form each half plate into a cone with the straight edges overlapping enough to give it stability. Tape it along the overlapped seam. Repeat with the other half plate.
4. Cut the ribbon into 12" (30.5 cm) strips.
5. Glue the ribbon inside the cone 1" (2.5 cm) from the top edge.
6. Let it dry thoroughly and fill with small gifts or candy. Tie a ribbon at the top.
7. Follow steps 5-6 to make a second *aguinaldo*.

Tin Ornament

In early Hispanic tradition, gold and silver were often used in making artwork because the metals were soft and easy to work with. However, as the value of these metals increased, artisans looked to other metals to replace gold and silver. When the Spanish forbade the natives to use the precious metals, the artisans began using tin. Now, many toys and ornaments are made from tin, often starting from simple scraps of metal that become transformed into beautiful works of art. Follow these directions to design a unique yet simple Christmas decoration.

Materials:

- Scrap paper
- Pencil
- Aluminum pie pan
- Craft paint pens
- Pen
- Scissors
- Hole punch
- Yarn or ribbon
- Tape
- Newspaper

Procedure:

1. Draw a detailed design on a piece of scrap paper to make a template for the ornament design.
2. Have an adult cut off the rim of the pie pan so that only a circle remains.
3. Tape the paper template to the circle, placing a few sheets of newspaper underneath.
4. Trace the pattern by pressing down very hard with a pen. Remove the pattern.
5. Let an adult cut the outside of the design to form the ornament.
6. Place the ornament on a surface with the pen marks facing down. Use craft paint pens to color the ornament between the raised lines.
7. Have an adult punch a hole at the top of the ornament.
8. Tie a piece of yarn or ribbon through the hole to display the completed ornament.

1.

2.
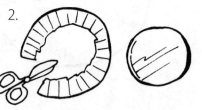

8.

5 - 7.

3 - 4.
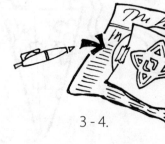

Materials:

- Paper lunch bag
- 2 cups of sand
- Votive candle
- Votive candle holder
- Markers
- Scissors

Teacher Note:
Caution: Never leave a burning candle unattended or within reach of children. Keep out of drafts. Do not move while lit or until wax hardens. Use caution when extinguishing.

Luminarias

Luminarias, which means little lanterns, are often used as a symbol to light the way for the Christ Child into homes on Christmas Eve. The original *luminaria* was a tall, even stack of kindling wood burned on the roof of a house. Today, people often use simple paper bags containing lit candles.

Procedure:

1. Fold the top edge of the bag down about 1½" (3.8 cm).
2. Draw a design on the bag.
3. Cut small slits on the top portion of the bag to allow the candlelight to show through.
4. Pour sand into the bag.
5. Place the candle in the candle holder, then place the holder in the sand. Press the candle holder into the sand to secure it.
6. Have an adult carefully light the candle.

Pedia de las Posada

This traditional song is often sung during the Christmas holiday season.

Nochebuena

This Christmas song celebrates Christmas Eve and makes mention of *buñuelos*, a popular, sweet treat.

Es - ta no - che es No - che - bue - na, no - che de co - mer bu - ñue - los,

no - che de lu - na, no - che de es - tre - llas pa - ra los ni - ños bue - nos.

The King's Bread

The Christmas celebration would not be complete without serving this recipe. An interesting note about this food is that the person who gets the piece of bread with the baby figurine is supposed to give a party on February 2, Candlemas Day.

INGREDIENTS:
Two loaves of prepared refrigerated yeast bread dough
Small porcelain figurine of a baby (must be able to safely withstand baking process)
Raisins, nuts, candied cherries, grated lemon, and orange peels

Separate the two dough loaves. Knead each loaf and place the figurine inside one loaf of dough. Add raisins, nuts, cherries, grated lemon, and orange peel to each loaf. Roll each loaf separately on a floured board into a ball. For each dough ball, twist the dough, forming a long piece, then join the two ends to form an oval ring. Cover and let the dough rings rise for about 30 minutes. Bake the loaves according to package directions. Drizzle icing over the top. (See below.)

ICING:
1½ tablespoons half-and-half
1 cup confectioners' sugar

Mix half-and-half with sugar until smooth. Drizzle mixture over the bread, allowing it to harden slightly.

Caution: Before completing any food activity, ask families' permission and inquire about students' food allergies and religious or other food preferences.

THE DAY OF THE INNOCENTS

One of the last Hispanic holidays of the year is The Day of the Innocents. Much like April Fools' Day, which occurs on April 1 in the United States, this holiday occurs in Mexico on December 28. It is a day set aside to honor children and to conduct fun, little pranks.

Besides holidays, there are many other days of the year set aside for parties or similar celebrations. This section contains information and activities about other special Hispanic events that call for *fiestas* (parties). Since food and music are often significant parts of many *fiestas*, pages 65-80 contain information, activities, recipes, and songs to duplicate Hispanic celebrations. Be sure to make each style of *piñata* described in this book because the *piñata* is a key element in many Hispanic parties, especially birthdays. Also try the various dishes and songs to make a truly festive Hispanic celebration!

This section contains information about:
- Baptisms
- Birthdays
- Weddings and Fifteenth Birthdays
- Food
- Music

BAPTISMS

In many early Hispanic tribal traditions, it was believed that when a baby was born, he was born sinful and needed to be purified. The Mayans, for example, conducted a special ceremony in which prayers and blessings were offered for all of the children born on the same day . Family and friends were invited to share in the festivities. After the ceremony, the families provided a feast for the guests.

After the Spanish introduced the native people to Catholicism, their baptism (*bautizo*) became a mixture of the church rituals blended with the ancient purification ceremonies. The babies were dressed in white, as was the custom of the Mayans, to signify purity and the promise of a bright future. Today, the baptism or christening is done in the church. According to Catholic tradition, the baby is freed from the original sin and is welcomed into the church family. The congregation of family and friends agrees to take responsibility to help raise the child in the church. The godmother and godfather, who have been selected with great care, agree to raise the child in the parents' absence.

At the baptism, the baby receives the name he will use. Traditionally, the baby's first name is the name of the saint who shares the same birthday. The baby's last name is comprised of the surnames of both parents. The order of the name is the first name (saint's name) followed by the father's surname and then the mother's surname.

Following the ceremony, food is served for all of those who attended. Traditional foods are served, along with plenty of sweets. Money is often given to the newly baptized child.

BIRTHDAYS

Traditionally, the birthday person is awakened on his birthday (*cumpleaños*) with a serenade to announce the beginning of the birthday celebration. A chorus of guitars, violins, and voices begin at dawn sounding the traditional birthday song "Las Mañanitas." A feast is held in honor of the birthday person.

On their birthdays, children celebrate with traditional *piñatas* filled with candies, small toys, and other treats. *Piñatas* come in various shapes and characters and are usually made from papier-mâché. A *piñata* is often hung from a tree branch. To open the *piñata*, each child is given a turn to be blindfolded. She is provided with a stick to hit the *piñata* and break it open. Once that happens, everyone runs and tries to grab as many treats as he can hold.

The Early Piñata

History tells us that the *piñata* did not originate in Mexico, but that it was brought to Mexico by Marco Polo from Italy. During the 16th and 17th centuries, the Italian nobility played a game called pignatta with a clay bowl filled with expensive items and hung on a rope. The object of the game was to break the clay pot and scramble for the riches. In Spain, it was transformed into a Lenten custom for all of the people. Clay pots were made in the shape of a pineapple and filled with candies. They were broken on the Sunday after Ash Wednesday.

In Mexico, there was a similar game. In December, the Aztecs celebrated the birth of their sun god, Huitzilopochtli. To commemorate his birthday, a clay pot was covered with feathers and filled with food. This clay pot was meant to represent evil. It was broken so that the food would fall at the feet of the idol that represented Huitzilopochtli. Since the Aztecs believed that their sun god was responsible for the sun rising each morning (demonstrating his power of good defeating evil), the breaking of the pot symbolized this event.

Paper Piñatas

There are many ways to make simple *piñatas* from everyday materials, such as paper bags.

Procedure:

1. Cut several 4" (10 cm) construction paper strips. Then, cut 2" (5 cm) slits into the strips.
2. Curl up each paper strip by rolling it around a pencil for about a minute.
3. Glue the paper strips to the grocery bag, making the bottom, closed end of the bag into the top.
4. Put candy and other small treats into the bag, filling it about halfway.
5. Close the bag by gathering the open end and tying it off with a piece of ribbon.
6. Hang the *piñata* by attaching string to the top of the bag and hanging it from the ceiling.

Materials:

- Construction paper (various colors)
- Paper grocery bag
- Pencil
- Scissors
- Ribbon
- Candy and/or small toys and treats

Materials:

- Paper lunch bags
- Piece of paper
- Pencil
- Scissors
- Glue
- Other craft materials (glitter, construction paper, crepe paper, etc.)
- Candy and/or small toys and treats
- Transparent tape

Paper Bag Piñata

This is a very simple *piñata* activity—and everyone gets her own small *piñata* to play with.

Procedure:

1. Cut a lunch bag in half across the middle.
2. Take a sheet of paper and fold it in half.
3. Draw a festive character with three distinct parts, such as the head, body, and tail of a parrot.
4. Cut out the parts. (Note: you will have two of each part.)
5. Glue the first parts (heads) to the sides of the bag where the opening is.
6. Glue the middle parts (bodies) to the sides of the bag and the end parts (tails) to the closed sides of the bag.
7. Decorate the bag with other craft materials appropriate to the design, such as crepe paper "feathers" for a parrot's tail.
8. Add candy and other small treats to the bag, filling it about halfway.
9. Close the open end of the bag with a few pieces of tape.
10. Hang the *piñata* by attaching string to the top of the bag and hanging it from the ceiling.

Balloon Piñata

This activity makes a *piñata* using a balloon as the form.

Procedure:

1. Tear the newspaper into several 4" (10 cm) strips.
2. Have an adult inflate and tie a balloon.
3. Dip the newspaper strips into the starch or glue mixture and wrap them around the balloon. Leave a small opening (approximately 2" (5 cm) in diameter) on the balloon uncovered.
4. Repeat step 3 three times. Allow each layer to dry before adding a new one.
5. Allow the *piñata* to dry completely.
6. Have an adult carefully pierce the balloon where it was left uncovered with a sewing needle. Then, cut a 2" (5 cm) hole.
7. Decorate the *piñata* with other craft materials to make it festive. For example, add construction paper eyes and a tail to make an animal.
8. Fill the *piñata* with candy and other small treats.
9. Cover the hole with a small piece of tape.

Materials:

- Newspaper
- Large, round balloon
- Glue and water mixture (1:1 ratio) or liquid starch
- Scissors
- Bowl
- Other craft materials (glitter, construction paper, crepe paper, etc.)
- Sewing needle
- Candy and/or small toys and treats
- Transparent tape

Teacher Note:
Caution: Before completing any balloon activity, ask families about possible latex allergies. Also, remember that uninflated or popped balloons may present a choking hazard.

Ándale amigo

This traditional song is often sung at birthday parties.

An - da - le a - mi - go, no te di - la - tes con la ca -

nas - ta de los ca - ca - hua - tes. An - da - le a - ci - ón.

Da - le, da - le, da - le, no pier - das el ti - no,

mi - de la dis - tan - cia que hay en el ca - mi - no

WEDDINGS AND FIFTEENTH BIRTHDAYS

The wedding (*boda*) and the fifteenth birthday (*quinceañera*) of a girl are grouped together because they are similar in many ways. In Hispanic culture, the entrance of a girl into adulthood is as precious and important as a woman entering into marriage. Both ceremonies are steeped in Catholic religious and other tradition and end with delicious food, festive music, and dancing into the night.

The *quinceañera* can be as costly as a wedding. Family and friends are asked to be responsible for certain arrangements for the event, such as the cake. Each person asked to help also pays for the item she helps with. This also happens for weddings, except the groom is responsible for most expenses. Both celebrations revolve around a special mass or ceremony. After the church ceremony, a feast follows that includes a special cake and many traditional Hispanic dishes and drinks.

Weddings do require some specific traditional preparations. For example, it is customary for the groom and his father to visit the bride's home many times prior to the wedding. With each visit, the subject of marriage is discussed and gifts are presented to show the groom's ability to provide for a new wife. Three weeks before the marriage, the bride and groom are presented to the priest. The day before the wedding, the bride and groom take part in communion and confession in a church.

FOOD

Food (*comida*) is a significant part of the many celebrations. Pages 73-76 contain recipes often served at a Hispanic table. Many recipes described in this section require an oven or stove, including the task of frying, and should be made prior to class and presented already prepared for young students to eat. For older students, copies of the recipes can be made and distributed to students for them to make at home (with family supervision). The completed dishes can be brought to school and served at a special class *fiesta* so that everyone can experience a variety of these delicious Hispanic foods!

Special Teacher Note:
Caution: Before completing any food activity, ask families' permission and inquire about students' food allergies and religious or other food preferences.

Los Bizcochitos

Note: Los Bizcochitos are similar to biscuits.
INGREDIENTS:
2 cups shortening
1 cup sugar
2 teaspoons anise seed
2 beaten egg yolks
1 teaspoon salt
6 cups flour
3 teaspoons baking powder
½ cup orange juice or water
2 tablespoons of cinnamon and sugar mixed together

Mix together shortening and sugar. Add anise seed and egg yolks. Sift together salt, flour, and baking powder. Gradually add small amounts of sifted dry ingredients and orange juice to the shortening mixture until all is well mixed into a doughy consistency. Roll dough to ⅛" (0.32 cm) thickness on a lightly floured board. Cut with cookie cutters, place on an ungreased cookie sheet, and bake for 8 to 10 minutes at 350°F (177°C) or until golden brown. Press the cookies into a cinnamon-sugar mixture while they are still warm.

Huevos Rancheros

Note: Huevos Rancheros is a dish which features eggs and a sauce.
INGREDIENTS:
6 corn tortillas
1 can of refried beans
6 fried eggs
1 jar of salsa
2 cups grated cheddar or Monterey Jack cheese

Gently warm each tortilla in a buttered frying pan on low heat for two minutes. Place the warm tortilla on a plate. On the tortilla, add a thin layer of refried beans. Then, place a fried egg on the tortilla and beans. Cover with salsa and grated cheese.

Churros

Note: Churros are fritters or crullers.
INGREDIENTS:
1 cup water
½ cup butter
1 cup flour
Dash of salt
3 eggs
Oil for frying
1 cup confectioners' sugar

Put water into a saucepan and bring to a boil. Add butter, and as soon as it melts, add the flour and salt. Stir over medium heat until it forms into a thick dough. Cool slightly, then beat in eggs one at a time until smooth. Put the smooth contents into a pastry bag with a star tip (or into a churros gun called a *churrero*) and squeeze in a continuous spiral into hot oil, which has been heated to 370°F (188°C). Remove each churro when brown, then drain on paper towels and sprinkle with sugar.

Buñuelos

Note: Buñuelos are crullers or fritters.

INGREDIENTS:

3 cups flour	1 teaspoon salt
½ cup shortening	3 eggs
Water	Oil for frying

Sift the flour and salt; work in shortening with fingers. Add eggs and just enough water to make a stiff dough and knead well. Form into balls and roll out ½" (1.3 cm) thick and round, like a tortilla. Let stand for a few minutes, then fry in hot oil, which has been heated to 390°F (199°C) until lightly browned and puffed. Drain on paper towels and serve with syrup. (See below.)

SYRUP:

2 cups brown sugar

1 cup of water

¼ teaspoon of crushed anise seed (or 1 teaspoon of cinnamon)

Warm brown sugar, water, and anise seed (or cinnamon) on medium heat, then drizzle warm sugar mixture over the buñuelos.

VARIATION:

To make sopaipillas, use the same recipe for making buñuelos except cut the dough into squares. After the sopaipillas are browned in the oil, drain them. Then, drizzle honey over the tops.

Hot Chocolate

The cocoa bean was very important to both the Mayans and Aztecs. Sometimes, it was used in place of money. But, they also used it in a simple but delicious drink. To make the drink, they roasted and ground the cocoa beans, then whipped the powder in hot water and flavored it with honey, vanilla, and other spices. Only the men of high rank were allowed to drink the chocolate because it was for royal and religious uses only. Columbus took the cocoa bean back to Spain in about 1502 where the royal court kept the chocolate secret to themselves. Today, Mexican chocolate often contains cinnamon, sugar, and ground almonds. Chocolate tablets are sold, cut into wedges, and placed into a pot with hot water or milk. It is then beaten with a special wooden instrument called a *molinillo*.

INGREDIENTS:
1 quart milk
¼ cup sugar
4 tablespoons cocoa
1 teaspoon cinnamon
Dash of salt

Heat milk to a near boil. Mix sugar, cocoa, cinnamon, and salt. Add the mix to the heated milk. Beat chocolate with a rotary beater or blender until frothy. Serve hot.

MUSIC

Music (*musica*) plays a key role in Hispanic *fiestas* (parties), as well as everyday life. Pages 77-80 contain a variety of commonly sung Hispanic songs.

El chocolate

This song that celebrates the treat of hot chocolate should be sung with the participants singing the song faster and faster as they rub their hands together, acting as if they are the *molinillo* (chocolate stirrer).

U - no, dos, tres, cho, U - no, dos, tres, co, U - no, dos, tres, la, U - no, dos, tres,

te. Cho - co - la - te, Cho - co - la - te, Ba - te, ba - te, cho - co - la - te.

Las mañanitas

This traditional song is often sung on the morning of a special day, such as a *cumpleaños* (birthday).

Es - tas son las ma - ña - ni - tas que can - ta-ba el rey Da - vid. Hoy que es

día de tu cum - ple a ños te las can - ta - mos a ti. Des -

pier - ta, mi bien, des - pier - ta, mi - ra que ya a-ma-ne - ció, ya los

pa - ja - ri - llos can - tan, la lu - na ya se me - tió.

Celebrating Hispanic Culture • CD-104040 • © Carson-Dellosa

La araña pequeñita

This fun children's song is known to many throughout the world. Encourage participants to use the well-known finger motions from "The Itsy Bitsy Spider" as they sing this version.

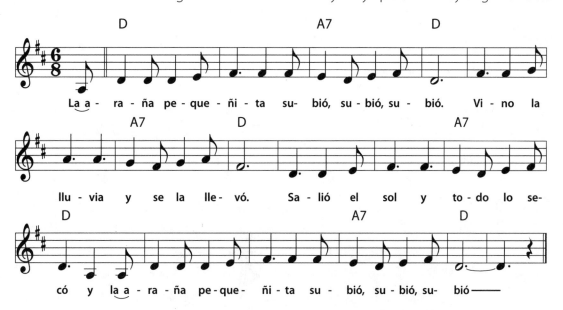

La a - ra - ña pe - que - ñi - ta su - bió, su - bió, su - bió. Vi - no la

llu - via y se la lle - vó. Sa - lió el sol y to - do lo se-

có y la a - ra - ña pe - que - ñi - ta su - bió, su - bió, su - bió ——

Duermete mi niño

This lullaby has helped many young Hispanic children drift off to sleep.

Duér - me - te, mi ni - ño duér - me - te so - li - to

que cuan - do des - pier - tes te da - ré a - to - li - to·